Sagebrush Psalms and Songs

Larry Chapman

BookLeaf Publishing

Presentation by *BookLeaf Publishing*

Web: www.bookleafpub.com

E-mail: info@bookleafpub.com

ISBN: 9789357613064

First edition 2022

*I would like to dedicate this to my wife
Linda, my 4 children and my 5
grandchildren and all those who have
encouraged and supported me. Thank you
and God Bless.*

ACKNOWLEDGEMENT

If anyone needs recognition or acknowledgement, it is my Heavenly Father. I have the easy job. He gave me the words and all I have to do is write them down.

PREFACE

In 2019, I suffered a near fatal heart attack. Since that time I very seriously pursued an active writing adventure. What I have accumulated in the last few years I feel I should share and hope many can enjoy.

Sound and Firm

When we build a sound foundation.
We have no room for earthly sensation.
We need to be eager to see what He has to show.
He will patiently tell us all the valuable things
we need to know.
On God's word we must depend.
It's length has no end.

Opportunity

God can free us from our sinful locks.
We must be ready when opportunity knocks.
We must have the desire to follow.
And no longer in sin continue to wallow.
On our Heavenly path we must not hesitate.
Our gracious Lord encourages us to participate.
What an absolutely glorious day it will be!!
When the gates of Heaven we get to see.
The gates of Heaven will never fall.
So in our quest we must never stall.

No Worries

On our behalf the Lord will defend.
A broken heart He can easily mend.
The Lord is well aware before we are.
To prevent damage that will leave a scar.
We may not have meant to offend.
But we are heard in the tone we send.

Plus and Minus

If negativity in our lives is allowed to consume.
On our daily Christian quest we must quickly resume.
On our journey we may encounter many foes.
Which was influenced by the lifestyle we chose.
Success is marked by the effort we exert.
If we choose pleasure instead of hurt.

No Losses

Nothing from our lives can be deducted.
As long as we follow what God has instructed.
Our God can take down an army of evil in
defeat.
To make our spiritual lives wholesomely
complete.
With our Lord there is no scarcity.
Consultation with the Lord will bring clarity.

A Will and A Way

By a dumpster he knelt on the ground.
Patiently eating something he had just found.
He did not seem unhappy or distraught.
He acted thankful for what he's got.
He picked up his tattered old pack.
And carefully slung it over his back.
In this bag is probably all he had.
But he did not appear disappointed or sad.
I followed at a distance to a large flat stone.
Where he could sit down and be all alone.
He reached into his pack and drew out a Book.
He calmly bowed his head and took a long look.
I could tell he held this Book ever so dear.
For on his wrinkled check a tear did appear.
I could tell from the expression on his face.
This was his very special time and place.
The lesson I learned here; the blessings I have to gain.
Will never be denied as long as I strive to attain.

Misery

Satan is like a pesky thorn.
He promotes constant misery and scorn.
When the stream of sin is deeper then I can ford.
I will submit willingly and plead my case to the
Almighty Lord.
A shield of protection my God will provide.
Through the darkness He will always guide.
The guarantee of God's eternal protection.
From the surroundings of gloom and rejection.

Broke

I woke up and looked on the floor.
That's all there is; there is none more.
That's about all I've got to share.
I am certain it's my last clean pair.
I pull these old britches on; one leg at a time.
I count my blessings even though I'm down to
my last dime.
I dig deep in my pocket.
Thankful for whatever I get.
I look around and see those that don't have
much.
But because of my faith, one day the pearly
gates I'll touch.

Excuses

Excuses are in our mind.
For solutions we can not find.
When we don't succeed we come up with an
excuse.
Because what God has shown us, we haven't put
to use.
An excuse is little more then an alibi.
Just another easier way to get by.
So many of our excuses come from our past.
We must rid them now or they will forever last.
To truly forgive is much more then to just to
forget.
It's a small portion our obligation has been met.

Security

Put a safety lock on your heart.
So the true feelings of love don't depart.
No greater Light can be found.
No more comforting Voice will sound.
The walk of our Christian faith is not a leap.
It is divinely designed for us to grasp and keep.
Our Lord rather we don't pretend.
What He shared, He did fully intend.

Creation is a Masterpiece

God is the greatest artist of all.
He illustrates winter, summer and fall.
My Lord just painted the most splendid
landscape.
From this beauty I don't want to ever escape.
I can look up at the gleaming sun.
And behold the creations He has done.
He hung the twinkling stars up so high.
To add luster and illuminate the cloudless sky.
There are no limits to my good Lords power.
Upon me all these wonderful blessings He did
shower.

Security

Put a safety lock on your heart.
So the true feelings of love don't depart.
No greater Light can be found.
No more comforting Voice will sound.
The walk of our Christian faith is not a leap.
It is divinely designed for us to grasp and keep.
Our Lord would rather we don't pretend.
What He shared He did fully intend.

Creation is a Masterpiece

God is the greatest artist of all.
He illustrates winter, summer and fall.
My Lord just painted the most splendid
landscape.
From this beauty I don't want to ever escape.
I can look up at the gleaming sun.
And behold the creations He has done.
He hung all the twinkling stars up so high.
To add luster and illuminate the cloudless sky.
There are no limits to my good Lords power.
Upon me all these wonderful blessings He did
shower.

Faith and Trust Are a Must

Might God is the only reason.
For each and every season.
No mortal being can take credit.
Only condemn and attempt to edit.
God's mighty blessings are His alone to oversee.
To be graciously distributed when we are
worthy.
There will be a glorious commotion.
When we all gather in spiritual devotion.
God's love will give us peace.
God's love for us will never cease.

Just a Fair Warning!!

There just is not enough earthly power available
today.
To ever try to take Our Lord and Savior away.
Simply because He will not submit to an evil
way.
He will not ever leave; He is here to stay.
Try as they may, try they might.
Our Lord will not disappear from sight.
Lock the Lord in your heart.
From there He will not depart.

Gone

On my gravestone don't say I'm dead.
I'm just upstairs sleeping in my Heavenly bed.
When you decide to come here.
Please do not shed a tear.
My work here on earth may be done.
But my life in Heaven has just begun.
Before I left there were a few things I didn't get
to say.
I'm sorry my Heavenly flight is leaving and I can
no longer stay.
I will see you sooner or later.
A little sooner would be greater.

Scoffer

We must constantly beware of the scoffer.
They are jealous of what we have to offer.
We must be conscious to realize.
Their opinions might be based on lies.
No way to know where this will lead.
But on a path of want; not need.

Any Doubt

Doubt will try to distort our Spiritual sight.
And detour our belief in our God's might.
Daily worldly temptations will constantly
attempt to frighten.
But our patient Lord is ever present to enlighten.
All God's blessings are a gift.
So from self destruction we may lift.
What our God has; He is so willing to give.
So in Heaven with Him we may forever live.

2 Parents

When important family decisions need to be
mutually decided.
Between a husband and wife they should be
evenly divided.
Children learn acceptable morals from parents of
two.
Christian structure will mold what they say and
do.
It is so vital when a family sits down to pray.
Because with all the negative temptation
spiritual believe is subject to decay.

A Will And A Way

By a dumpster he knelt on the ground.
Patiently eating something he had just found.
He did not seem unhappy or distraught.
He acted thankful for what he's got.
He picked up his tattered old pack.
And carefully slung it over his back.
In this bag is probably all he had.
But he did not appear disappointed or sad.
I followed at a distance to a large flat stone.
Where he could sit down and be all alone.
He reached into his pack and drew out
 a book.
He calmly bowed his head and look a long look.
I could tell he held this book ever so dear
For on his wrinkled cheek a tear did appear.
I could tell from the expression on his face.
This was his very special time and place.
The lesson I learned here; the blessings
I have to gain.
Will never be denied as long as I strive to attain.

More Than a Reminder

Our Lord God is not hesitant to remind.
That if we frequently seek we will find.
If his word we fully embrace.
Sin will disappear without a trace.
His love was sent from the heavens above.
With the full content of his precious love.
Our God never asks us to repay.
In our hearts he wants love to stay.

9 789357 613064